FOR BRIGITTE SCHRAN BROWN, DEAR FRIEND AND EXPERT TRANSLATOR.
FOR MY "SPYSTERS," SUSAN PEARSON, DARRIN JAYNE, AND LINDA FORTUNE.
AND FOR MR. HISTORY, KYLE CREWS.—*M.V.*

FOR MY STUDENTS AT IWU—BE STRONG AND ALWAYS COURAGEOUS.—*R.M.*

This story is true to the facts of Irena Sendler's life and the times during which she lived. It is a narrative biography in which some imagined scenes, people, thoughts, and dialogue have been included. These parts of the story are dramatic extensions of historically documented events and interactions.

Thank you to Severin Hochberg, historian formerly at the Center for Advanced Holocaust Studies at the United States Holocaust Memorial Museum for seventeen years and currently teaching history at George Washington University, for reviewing this story and for his valuable input.

Text copyright © 2011 by Marcia Vaughan • Illustrations copyright © 2011 by Ron Mazellan
LEE & LOW BOOKS Inc., 95 Madison Avenue, New York, NY 10016
leeandlow.com
Manufactured in Singapore by Tien Wah Press, September 2011
Book design by Kimi Weart, with additional design by David and Susan Neuhaus/NeuStudio
Book production by The Kids at Our House
The text is set in 13-point Rotis Semi-Serif
The illustrations are rendered in oil on canvas
10 9 8 7 6 5 4 3 2 1
First Edition
Library of Congress Cataloging-in-Publication Data
Vaughan, Marcia K.
Irena's jars of secrets / by Marcia Vaughan ; illustrated by Ron Mazellan.
p. cm.
Summary: "The story of Irena Sendler, a Polish Catholic social worker who helped rescue nearly 2,500 Jewish children from the Warsaw Ghetto in Nazi-occupied Poland during World War II. Includes afterword, sources, and glossary"—Provided by publisher.
ISBN 978-1-60060-439-3 (hardcover : alk. paper)
1. Sendlerowa, Irena, 1910-2008—Juvenile literature. 2. Righteous Gentiles in the Holocaust—Poland—Biography—Juvenile literature.
3. World War, 1939-1945—Jews—Rescue—Poland—Juvenile literature. 4. Holocaust, Jewish (1939-1945)—Poland—Juvenile literature.
5. Jewish children in the Holocaust—Poland—Warsaw—Juvenile literature. 6. Jews—Poland—Warsaw—History—20th century—Juvenile literature.
7. World War, 1939-1945—Poland—Warsaw—Juvenile literature. 8. Warsaw (Poland)—Biography—Juvenile literature. I. Mazellan, Ron. II. Title.
D804.66.S46V38 2011   940.53'18092—dc22   [B]   2011016386

IRENA'S JARS of SECRETS

by **Marcia Vaughan**   *illustrated by* **Ron Mazellan**

LEE & LOW BOOKS INC. • NEW YORK

On a cold February day in 1910, a baby girl was born to a Catholic family in a small town near Warsaw, Poland. Her parents named their daughter Irena and raised her to respect all people, regardless of their religion or race.

When Irena was seven years old, a typhus epidemic broke out in Warsaw. Irena's father was the only doctor in the area who would treat poor Jewish patients, but soon he too came down with the disease. As he lay dying, he held his daughter's hand and told her that if she ever saw someone drowning, she must jump in and try to save that person, even if she could not swim.

Irena never forgot her father's words and his dedication to helping those in need.

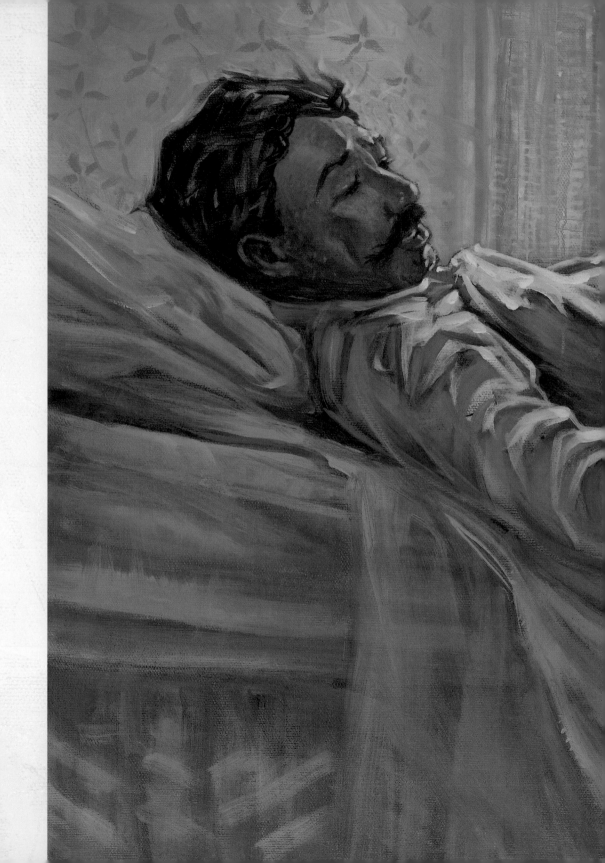

In 1939 Adolf Hitler's German army invaded Poland. This was the start of World War II. Hitler, leader of the Nazi Party, intended to control all of Europe under German rule and eliminate the races, minorities, and other groups that he believed were inferior to the Germans. At the top of Hitler's list were the Jews, whom he saw as enemies of Germany and partly to blame for the country's defeat in World War I.

More than four hundred thousand Jews lived in the Warsaw area. Late in 1940 German soldiers forced these Jews into the Warsaw Ghetto, a neighborhood of rundown apartment buildings that was sealed off by a high brick wall. Trapped inside, the people awaited their fate at the hands of those who had imprisoned them.

Irena, now a social worker, remembered her father's words from many years ago. *The Jewish people are drowning,* she thought; and she knew in her heart that she had to help them.

One day Irena approached a ghetto entrance.

"Halt!" snapped the guard, raising his rifle. "No one is allowed in or out of the ghetto."

Irena, wearing the uniform of a nurse, held out papers from the epidemic control department. "I have permission to enter to investigate an outbreak of typhus," she said.

Entering the ghetto was like entering a nightmare. The people inside were struggling to survive. They did not have enough food, water, medicine, or heating fuel.

Irena's heart filled with grief. As she walked through the ghetto, hungry children cried out. People lay sick and starving in the streets. Everywhere Irena turned, she saw death and despair.

For the next two years Irena went to the ghetto often. *The food, clothes, and medicine I smuggle in are not enough,* she thought bitterly. Everyone was suffering, especially the children. Irena felt she must do more.

In 1942 the Nazis began sending Jews to Treblinka, an extermination camp about sixty miles from Warsaw. In a race to save as many children as possible, Irena joined Zegota, a secret organization that was helping Jews in Poland survive and find places of safety. Irena became head of the children's department and, along with other Zegota members, came up with clever ways to smuggle children out of the ghetto.

But first Irena had to convince Jewish parents to let their children be taken away and placed with non-Jewish families or organizations outside the ghetto.

Like most families, the Wolmans did not want to give up their child.

"Is it better for Elka to suffer and starve behind these walls?" Irena asked. "And what will happen when the soldiers come to send you to the camp at Treblinka?"

"The Nazis say no harm will come to us there," Mr. Wolman argued.

"That's a lie," Irena told him. "The people who go there are killed."

Mrs. Wolman's face was wet with tears. "If we give you our daughter, can you promise us she'll live?"

"No," Irena said. "But if she stays here she will surely die."

"How will we get back together when the war is over?" Mr. Wolman asked.

"I'll keep your child's real name and new identity on a secret list so you can find her," Irena promised the worried parents.

Suddenly the door downstairs slammed open, and the sound of soldiers' boots pounding on the front steps echoed upstairs.

"They're coming!" Mrs. Wolman cried. "Take her!"

The Wolmans quickly kissed Elka good-bye. The child cried out as Irena took Elka from her mother's arms and hurried away through the hall and down the back stairway.

One day Irena and another member of Zegota hid a baby under the floorboards of the ambulance they were driving out of the ghetto. Riding between them was a dog.

"I see you come here two, sometimes three, times a day," a guard at the gate said to Irena. "I want to see what you've got in there."

At that moment the child whimpered, and Irena's heart froze. If the guard found the baby, they would all be shot. So Irena hit the dog on its paw. Immediately the dog began to bark, drowning out the child's sounds.

"Shut that dog up before I put a bullet in it!" snapped the guard, and he waved them through the gate.

As they drove away, Irena patted the dog's head. Their secret passenger had been saved.

Older children understood the need for silence, secrecy, and deception.

"Rivka," Irena said, "if you can pretend to be very sick, we'll take you out in the ambulance; and we'll hide your little brother, Aaron, under your stretcher." Then Irena warned Aaron that no matter what happened, he must not make a sound.

At the exit gate a guard threw open the door of the ambulance.

"This girl does not look sick to me," he shouted, jabbing her with his rifle.

Instead of crying in pain, Rivka moaned as if she were very ill. But the terror was too much for Aaron. He began to sob. To cover the sound, Rivka began coughing.

"Don't get too close unless you want to catch typhus," the ambulance driver warned.

"Typhus?" The guard backed away. "Get her out of here at once!"

On other trips into the ghetto, Irena and her Zegota team carried babies and young children out in baskets, boxes, tool chests, sacks, and suitcases. When garbage was removed from the ghetto, children were sometimes hidden on the truck under piles of trash. Escapes with older children were made through the sewers or old courthouse, or by bribing the guards to let them escape.

Once the children were out of the ghetto they were given new identity papers and taken to live in orphanages, convents, or non-Jewish foster homes. It was not easy to find families who were willing to pretend that a Jewish child was one of their own. Yet people did come forward, ready to help save the lives of innocent children.

As she had promised, Irena kept lists of the children's real and false identities so they could be reunited with their families after the war. She placed the lists in jars, which were buried under an apple tree in a friend's garden. As more children were rescued, Irena dug up the jars, added their names to the lists, and buried the jars again.

In October 1943 Irena was betrayed to the Germans. They were told that she was smuggling children out of the ghetto. Irena was arrested by the Gestapo, the German secret police, and taken to Pawiak prison.

One day a Gestapo officer entered Irena's cell. "You tell us the whereabouts of every child you helped escape and the names of your collaborators," he demanded, "or you will die."

If Irena told the Germans the location of the buried jars, she knew that the children, the people who sheltered them, and those who assisted her would all be killed. Over the next three months the police beat and tortured her, but Irena kept her silence.

And so she was sentenced to death.

As Irena awaited execution, she felt strangely at peace. Although she would die, she knew many others would live.

The day after Irena was to be killed, posters that hung all over Warsaw listed Irena Sendler among the people who had been shot by a firing squad. The Gestapo did not know that at the last moment members of Zegota had paid a bribe. Instead of being shot, Irena had secretly been set free.

When the Gestapo later learned of the deception, they sent search parties to look for Irena. But like the children she helped rescue, Irena went into hiding. Using a new identity, she continued to work with Zegota from her hiding places. The Gestapo never found her.

After World War II ended in 1945, Irena returned once again to the apple tree. She dug down through the dirt and rocks in the garden and uncovered the jars and their precious contents. Irena counted the names. On her lists were about twenty-five hundred Jewish children who had been rescued.

Irena gave the lists to the Jewish National Committee, which found that most of the children had survived the war. But Irena's hopes of reuniting them with their families faded as she learned that nearly all of the parents had died in extermination camps. Using the information in Irena's lists, the committee found living relatives for some children. Other children stayed with their non-Jewish families, and some children went to live in other countries.

Irena Sendler never thought of herself as a hero. She only did what she felt she must, and wished she could have done more.

"Every child saved with my help and the help of all the wonderful secret messengers, who today are no longer living, is the justification of my existence on this earth, and not a title to glory."

—*Irena Sendler,*
from a letter to the Polish Senate, 2007

AFTERWORD

Irena Sendler was twenty-nine years old when World War II began in 1939. As a senior administrator in the Warsaw Social Welfare Department, she helped care for the growing numbers of poor people. The Jews, especially, were in great need because the German occupying forces had taken their homes, their money, and their belongings. Defying German orders, Irena and her coworkers registered Jewish families under Christian names so they could receive aid.

When the Jewish population was imprisoned in the Warsaw Ghetto in October and November 1940, few knew that almost all these men, women, and children would eventually be sent to Treblinka, an extermination camp being built in northeastern Poland. When it became clear what the Germans intended, Irena joined the underground organization Zegota, the Council for Aid to Jews. Using the code name Jolanta and a pass from the Contagious Disease Department, Irena gained entry into the ghetto to check sanitary conditions. This gave her and her network of social workers and rescuers a chance to sneak in food, medicine, and money. Even though the work was extremely dangerous, they also managed to smuggle children past the Nazi guards and out of the ghetto.

"We would go to the ghetto and try to get as many children as possible because the situation would worsen every day," Irena Sendler said later.

Irena and her Zegota workers told the foster families and organizations that the Jewish children they agreed to care for must be reunited with their parents or relatives when the war ended. She kept careful records of each child's Jewish name and false identity on two identical lists. These were kept in two glass jars and buried under an apple tree in a friend's garden across the street from the German soldiers' barracks. The secrecy of this information was vital to the survival of the children and all who helped them.

World War II ended in 1945. Germany had been defeated, but not before millions of people in Europe had been murdered, including six million Jews. One and one-half million of those were children. This systematic killing by the Germans and their allies is known as the Holocaust.

When Irena's lists were dug up for the last time, they contained the names of approximately twenty-five hundred rescued children, although the exact number is not known.

For many years Poland's Communist government ignored Irena's story and the stories of other brave Polish people who helped Jews during the war. But Irena's selfless deeds were recognized in 1965 by Yad Vashem, the Jewish people's memorial to the Holocaust. Irena Sendler was honored as Righteous Among the Nations, a title given to non-Jews who risked their own lives to save Jewish people during the Holocaust. In 1991 she was made an honorary citizen of Israel. After the fall of Poland's Communist government, in 2003 Irena was awarded the Order of the White Eagle, Poland's highest honor. That year she was also given the Jan Karski Freedom Award for Valor and Compassion by Freedom House and the American Center of Polish Culture. And in 2007 Irena Sendler was nominated for the Nobel Peace Prize. When her photograph appeared in the newspapers, people began to call. "I remember your face," the callers said. "It was you who took me out of the ghetto."

Irena Sendler spent the last years of her life in a nursing home in Warsaw. She was cared for by Elzbieta Ficowska, who as a baby had been smuggled out of the ghetto in a carpenter's box hidden under a load of bricks.

In 2008, at the age of ninety-eight, Irena Sendler was one of the last surviving members of the children's department of Zegota. Although she passed away on May 12 of that year, her story of caring and courage lives on.

Glossary and Pronunciation Guide

Adolf Hitler (AD-olf HIT-ler): Chancellor of Germany from 1933 to 1945; leader of the National Socialist German Workers' Party (Nazi Party)

ally (AL-eye): person, group, or country that gives aid and/or support to another

Catholic (KATH-lik *or* KAH-thuh-lik): person who is a member of the Roman Catholic church

convent (KON-vent): building where a group of people devoted to religious life live; usually used by Catholic nuns

epidemic (eh-puh-DEH-mik): outbreak of disease that spreads very quickly and affects a large number of people

extermination camp (ek-STUR-muh-nay-shuhn kamp): place where large numbers of people are sent to be killed; during World War II, the Nazis sent people they considered enemies or undesirable to extermination camps

firing squad (FYER-ing skwahd): group of soldiers assigned to shoot a prisoner who has been sentenced to death

Gestapo (geh-STAH-poh): official secret police force of Nazi Germany known for its brutal methods

ghetto (GET-oh): poor, run-down part of a city where people of the same race, religion, or ethnic background live; during World War II, many Jews in Poland were forced to live in the Warsaw Ghetto

Holocaust (HOH-luh-kost): systematic killing of millions of Jews and other minorities and groups in Europe by the Germans and their allies during World War II

Irena Sendler (eye-REN-ah SEND-ler): Polish Catholic social worker who helped rescue about 2,500 Jewish children during World War II

Jew (joo): person who practices the religion of Judaism

Jewish (JOO-ish): having to do with Jews, their religion, or their culture

Jewish National Committee (JOO-ish NASH-nuhl kuh-MI-tee): group of organizations that helped Jews in Poland during and after World War II

Nazi (NOT-see *or* NAT-see): member of the National Socialist German Workers' Party, led by Adolf Hitler, that ruled Germany from 1933 to 1945; Nazis believed in German racial superiority and attempted to rid the world of people they considered enemies or undesirable

Pawiak (PAH-vee-ahk): prison in Warsaw, Poland; used by the Gestapo during World War II to hold and torture prisoners

Poland (POH-luhnd): country in central Europe; the invasion of Poland by Germany in 1939 caused the start of World War II

social worker (SOH-shuhl WUR-kur): person who works helping others with problems related to health, housing, poverty, unemployment, disabilities, and other social issues

Treblinka (TRUH-bling-kuh): Nazi extermination camp that existed from 1942 to 1943 near Warsaw, Poland, where about 800,000 Jews were put to death during World War II

typhus (TYE-fuhs): serious infectious disease that is spread by lice and fleas and that causes intense headache, high fever, and a dark red rash

Warsaw (WOR-saw): capital of Poland; during World War II the city was occupied by German troops and subjected to systematic destruction

World War II (wurld wor too): war fought mainly in Europe, Asia, and North Africa from 1939 to 1945

Zegota (zhyeh-GOH-tah): code name for the Council for Aid to Jews; Polish non-Jewish underground organization that assisted Jewish people and found places of safety for them from 1942 to 1945 during World War II

Author's Sources

Books

Ackerman, Diane. *The Zookeeper's Wife: A War Story*. New York: W. W. Norton & Company, 2007.

Anflick, Charles. *Resistance: Teen Partisans and Resisters Who Fought Nazi Tyranny*. New York: Rosen Publishing Group, 1999.

Downing, David. *Toward Genocide*. World Almanac Library of the Holocaust. Milwaukee, WI: World Almanac Library, 2005.

Haas, Gerda. *These I Do Remember: Fragments from the Holocaust*. Freeport, ME: Cumberland Press, 1982.

Mieszkowska, Anna. *Die Mutter der Holocaust-Kinder*. Translated for the author of this story by Brigitte Schran Brown. Munich, Germany: Verlagsgruppe Random House, 2004.

Rymkiewicz, Jaroslaw M., and Nina Taylor, trans. *The Final Station: Umschlagplatz*. New York: Farrar, Straus & Giroux, 1994.

Stewart, Gail B. *Life in the Warsaw Ghetto*. San Diego: Lucent Books, 1995.

Zullo, Allan, and Mara Bovsun. *Survivors: True Stories of Children in the Holocaust*. New York: Scholastic Inc., 2004.

Web Sites and Media

Bülow, Louis. "Irena Sendler: An Unsung Heroine." The Holocaust: Crimes, Heroes and Villains. http://www.auschwitz.dk/Sendler.htm.

Gessner, Peter K. "Irena Sendler: WWII Rescuer and Hero." InfoPoland, University at Buffalo. http://info-poland.buffalo.edu/classroom/sendler/index.html.

Harrison, John Kent, and Lawrence John Spagnola. *The Courageous Heart of Irena Sendler*. Directed by John Kent Harrison. Hallmark Hall of Fame. Released April 19, 2009. DVD, 95 min.

Hevesi, Dennis. "Irena Sendler, Lifeline to Young Jews, Is Dead at 98." *New York Times* online, May 13, 2008. http://www.nytimes.com/2008/05/13/world/europe/13sendler.html.

"Irena Sendler: 1910–2008." Jewish Virtual Library. http://www.jewishvirtuallibrary.org/jsource/biography/irenasendler.html.

Irena Sendler: In the Name of Their Mothers. Produced and directed by Mary Skinner. PBS/KQED Public Television. San Francisco: 2B Productions. Aired May 1, 2011. Released June 7, 2011. DVD, 60 min.

Life In a Jar: The Irena Sendler Project. http://www.irenasendler.org/.

Life In a Jar: The Irena Sendler Project. Funded by the Milken Family Foundation and Lowell Milken Center. Fort Scott, KS, 1992. DVD.

Polonsky, Antony. "Irena Sendler: Polish social worker who saved around 2,500 Jewish children from the Nazis." *The Guardian* online, May 14, 2008. http://www.guardian.co.uk/world/2008/may/14/secondworldwar.poland.

"Smuggling Children out of the Ghetto: Irena Sendler, Poland." Yad Vashem: The Righteous Among The Nations. http://www1.yadvashem.org/righteous_new/poland/sendler.html.

Snyder, Don. "Holocaust heroine recalled by two she saved." msnbc.com, September 24, 2008. http://worldblog.msnbc.msn.com/archive/2008/09/24/1438429.aspx.

Tomaszewski, Irene, and Tecia Werbowski. "Chapter 4: The Konrad Zegota Committee." Zegota. Project InPosterum: Preserving the Past for the Future. http://www.projectinposterum.com/docs/zegota.htm.

United States Holocaust Memorial Museum. http://www.ushmm.org/.

Woo, Elaine. "Irena Sendler, 1910–2008: WWII savior of young Jews." *Los Angeles Times* online, May 13, 2008. http://articles.latimes.com/2008/may/13/local/me-sendler13.